Let's Count Apples

Contemos Manzanas

Sharon Marie White

To order additional copies of this book, contact:
Xlibris
844-714-8691
www.Xlibris.com
Orders@Xlibris.com

Interior Image Credit: Arsalan Khan

ISBN: Softcover   978-1-5245-6027-0
       EBook   978-1-5245-6026-3

Library of Congress Control Number: 2016919158

Print information available on the last page

Rev. date: 01/27/2021

Illustrations by Arsalan Khan

In Loving Memory of my Father,
Charles Ray White

Dedicated to my Mother,
Lois Marie Allen

Charles

Lois

1

One   White

Uno   Blanca

El árbol blanco de manzanas tiene una manzana.

The white tree has one apple.

2

Two   Purple

Dos   Murado

El árbol morado tiene dos manzanas.

The purple tree has two apples.

3

Three   Orange

Tres   Naranja

El árbol naranja tiene tres manzanas.

The orange tree has three apples.

4

Four   Pink

Cuatro   Rosado

El árbol rosado tiene cuatro manzanas.

The Pink tree has four apples.

5

Five

Red

Cinco

Rojo

El árbol rojo tiene cinco manzanas.

The red tree has five apples.

6

Six

Green

Seis

Verde

El árbol verde tiene seis manzanas.

The green tree has six apples.

Seven   Brown

Siete   Café

El árbol café tiene siete manzanas.

The brown tree has seven apples.

8

Eight

Blue

Ocho

Azul

El árbol azul tiene ocho manzanas.

The blue tree has eight apples.

9

Nine   Yellow

Nueve   Amarillo

El árbol Amarillo tien mueve manzanas.

The yellow tree has nine apples.

10

Ten

Black

Diez

Negro

El árbol negro tiene diez manzanas.

The black tree has ten apples.

Numbers   Números

1	One	Uno
2	Two	Dos
3	Three	Tres
4	Four	Cuatro
5	Five	Cinco
6	Six	Seis
7	Seven	Siete
8	Eight	Ocho
9	Nine	Nueve
10	Ten	Diez

Colors   Colores

red	rojo
purple	morado
orange	naranja
pink	rosado
green	verde
brown	café
blue	azul
yellow	amarillo

Printed in the United States
By Bookmasters